UX/UI DESIGN 2021 FOR BEGINNERS

A Simple Approach to UX/UI Design for Intuitive Designers

DAVID WEATHERS

Copyright

All rights reserved. No part of this book may be reproduced or used in any manner without the prior written permission of the copyright owner, except for the use of brief quotations in a book review.

While the advice and information in this book are believed to be true and accurate at the date of publication, neither the authors nor the editors nor the publisher can accept any legal responsibility for any errors or omissions that may be made. The publisher makes no warranty, express or implied, with respect to the material contained herein.

Printed in the United States of America
© 2021 by David Weathers

Table of Contents

Copyright i

Introduction 1

Chapter 1 2

Getting the terms right 2

What does UX and UI mean? 2

What is UI? 2

What is UX? 3

The Differences between the UX and UI 4

Which comes first in the design process? 5

What are the different effects of UX and UI designs in web pages and applications? ... 6

Chapter 2 8

Getting started – Choosing, Practicing and mastering a design tool 8

Choosing a design tool 8

Practicing and mastering the design tool 9

Chapter 3 11

Researching 11

Creating surveys 11

Steps to create an effective survey 11

Tools for creating surveys online 14

Involving colleagues, stakeholders and partners in the design process 17

How different individuals might use the product or service 17

One on one interviews... 18

Chapter 4.. 19

Brainstorming... 19

Compiling your research and putting them together... 19

Drafting diagrams of proposed user steps 21

Drafting wireframes... 21

Creating a Prototype.. 23

Chapter 5.. 25

Bringing the UI designer into the picture 25

Chapter 5.. 29

Implementation and Design 29

Frontend development and its languages................. 29

Overview on HTML, CSS and JavaScript 29

Backend Development 31

Chapter 6 32

Testing 32

Qualitative and quantitative user research 32

Usability testing 32

Tips to getting a good usability testing 33

Types of usability testing 34

Iterative testing 36

Advantages of Iterative testing 37

Steps to making a good iterative testing 37

Signs of a good UX design 38

Signs of a good UI design 40

Chapter 7 43

Designing the ideal digital product 43

Making users the center of your design using UCD ... 43

Taking a mobile first strategy 44

Focusing on quality rather than quantity 46

Information architecture (IA) 49

Why you should be a UX and UI designer 51

Chapter 8 53

The user Interface 53
How graphic design knowledge helps in UI design 53
Using breathtaking images 54
Effects of colors and font 55
Responsive and adaptive design 57
Responsive design 57
Adaptive design 58
Creating equal accessibility to all users 60
Chapter 9 62
The Kaizen concept 62
What is the Kaizen Concept? 62
Improvement through feedback 63
Working toward improvement rather than
perfection 64
Reasons to aim for improvement rather than
perfection 65
Conclusion 67
About the Author 69

Introduction

For a long time, there has been a debate as to what these terms really mean in the digital design industry. So many have confused it to be the same thing and they are often used interchangeably and sometimes together to mean the same thing. Even employers do not often know the difference between these two when hiring designers. However, it is important for us to note that these two terms differ in the creation and design of digital products. In large companies, teams are often used to share work among specialists and this is where the different fields come into play. As a UX designer, you can also be a UI designer but the specialists in UI design often stand out when it comes to excellent designs.

Chapter 1

Getting the terms right

What does UX and UI mean?

What is UI?

UI is short for user interface and it refers to the outward display and visual looks of the digital product. It is the graphical layout of the web page or application where you have the buttons, pictures, colors font, touch points and the general looks of the page. The UI design also includes how the product is displayed in various devices such as phones, tablets and Computers.

UI design is generally where human and machine interaction happen. Here you have the controls, which are used to operate the product. When you scroll through a webpage using your up or down control, a user interface is letting you do that.

UI designers generally have knowledge in graphics design and photography. This makes them able to create tools that when integrated into the webpage or application, brings out the beauty in it. An example of such tools is the graphical user interface, which makes use of images and visual elements to enable the user to interact with the product.

You get to interact with a product through touch points, which are created by UI designers. UI designs give users the first impression when they use a website or app. These designs influence the user's actions mostly. Using some text, pictures and colors can motivate users to stay longer and consume more content from a digital product.

What is UX?

UX on the other hand is how the digital product feels to the user. This includes how the buttons work, how pages are loaded and how easy or hard it is to navigate through pages. The user experience of a website is determined by the effectiveness of the UX design. This design is often targeted at making this experience a satisfying one to the user.

UX designers generally focus on priorities such as movement from different pages, the speed and time it takes to do this, how to make the navigation journey easy.

Nobody would want to come back to a stressful product regardless of the information they may find there. This often happens in products where navigation is a very difficult thing to do.

Two great ways to put these terms;

- UI is how good the car looks. UX is how you feel driving it.
- UI is how good the pizza looks. UX is how it tastes like when you eat it.

The Differences between the UX and UI

UX	UI
Focuses on the overall experience of the user: This could include how the user navigates from a product home page to the sales or buying page of the digital design.	**Focuses on the visuals and touch points of the product:** These visuals include buttons, status bar icons, background picture, text font/ size/ color, page background color among others.
Operation: UX designers focus on how the commands are being implemented in the	**Adaptability and responsiveness**: They are responsible for making the User Interface look

product.	good on all devices.
UI design is more analytical.	UI is graphical.
UX makes the product more enjoyable and easy to use.	UI makes the product more attractive to the eyes.

Which comes first in the design process?

In designing the digital product, the UX designer starts by taking a couple of actions, which are going to be discussed in subsequent chapters of this book. The start of every digital product is the research process and some other related actions all of which are carried out by the UX designer. The UI designer comes in at a point when the UX designer has put the skeleton of the design and its structure in place. However, the UI designer can make some modifications to the entire work. This is to say that the UX designer and the UI designer must work closely together to make sure the product is its best. All the unseen engineering done by the UX designer is brought to life by the UI designer who creates interfaces such as buttons and options to communicate with them. Hence, the UX design is the beginning of the digital product.

What are the different effects of UX and UI designs in web pages and applications?

Both designs go a long way in determining the success of a website or application. You could get bad reviews on either your products or good ones. In this case, the praises and criticism always go to these designers.

It is the primary goal of businesses to drive more sales and increase its customers, which is why the web app or application was designed in the first place. The UI and UX designs put together makes this happen but let's look at the individual effects these designs have on the product.

UI designs

As earlier stated, the UI design is the first impression you take from the product. When you go to a web page or launch an app, you get colors and then touch points such as a sign in option, a text field where you can type in your username and password and a login button. This visible interface, which helps you communicate with the machine or prod-uct, is the UI design. Without it, the product is a gun without a trigger.

UX designs

This design determines if the customer comes back or not. Like in the majority of life endeavors, businesses and others, appearance moves people but the behavior and experience they get is the deciding factor for the next patronage. The beauty of a car attracts a buyer but the experience gotten from the car determines if there is going to be a deal or not. It is the same in websites and apps. In this case, the UX designer's goal is to make sure the user gets the best experience using the product, as this is important to future patronage. UX designers often put users in mind when creating designs. This helps to create easy to use products.

Chapter 2

Getting started – Choosing, Practicing and mastering a design tool

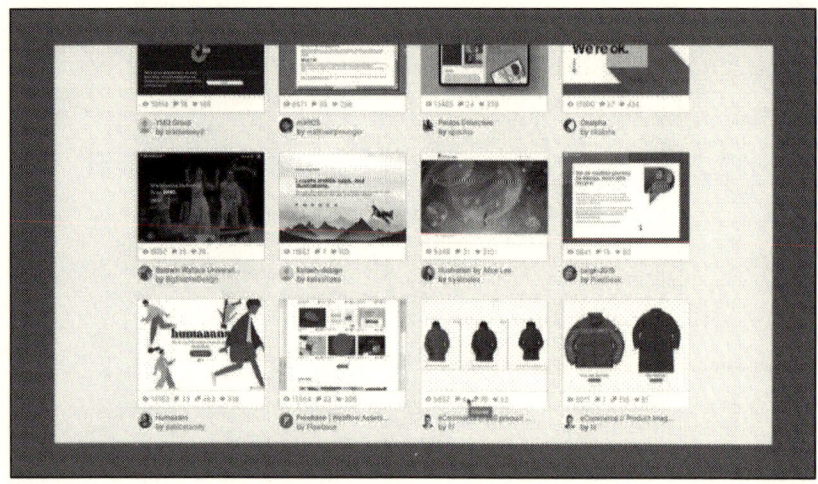

Choosing a design tool

To get started on your design process, you have to first choose a design tool to help you carry out your project designs. Some design tools you can check out include Figma, Adobe XD or Sketch. These are tools that come with the features you need for your design. You can use a free plan with limited features or unlock all features by going premium. Both work on all computers.

One of the most effective design tools is Figma and since it offers free access, it is the most popular tool among UX and UI designers. We are going to be looking at Figma but you can also choose another design tool that best suits your needs.

Practicing and mastering the design tool

You want to start practicing your designs by copying other designs so you can always have a reference to fall back to when you encounter a challenge. This will give you a little experience when you eventually start building your own product from scratch.

- To start, go to www.figma.com and click on the **sign up** option to create an account. It is free for individuals.
- Search for free Figma resources from Google and copy them to your figma account so you can start your practicing. You just need the templates for practicing and it does not necessarily mean you are going to be using them for official purposes.

- Copy the resource to your figma account and start your practicing. Learn more about about Figma, on https://help.figma.com/hc/en-us/categories/360002051613-Get-started

Chapter 3

Researching

Creating surveys

This is the first step to the research process and it involves throwing questions to the general public to get an idea of what the people are talking about, how they are feeling and then recording and gathering their replies to understand what they really want. Surveys can be anonymous and are usually conducted as either open or closed surveys. The open survey is one where the users give direct and completely personal answers to questions using text or writings while the closed survey comes with some fixed options you can choose from. These options could be checkboxes, radio buttons and even yes or no options. In open surveys, the user answers how they want to while in closed surveys, the users answers according to the options provided.

Steps to create an effective survey

- **Understanding the goal of the survey:** First, you have to take note that the goal of the

survey is to understand the problems and their present position of the users in order to create the desired changes to better serve them.
- **Understanding the current and future position of the users:** you have to also take note of the present position of your users so you can know how to build your product to improve their current condition, overcome their obstacles and help them get to their desired future position.
- **Asking the right questions:** it is also important to ask your users the right questions to get the right answers. Do not mix questions and be as straightforward as possible.

  Your questions should include their current and desired position, their current and desired cost, their current and desired competition, their concerns, obstacles, and their general goals.
- **Targeting the right audience:** knowing the people your product is going to serve and targeting them with your surveys is the right way to get the best opinions to make your work the best it can be. An example is in the

case is when creating an app to organize courses for students from different grades. In this case, your surveys should be targeted at students. This is the way to get the most relevant answers to help build the product.
- **Avoiding Partial/biased questions and options:** If you are using a closed survey, be sure not to ask questions or provide options that are simply geared toward achieving a particular reply. For instance, giving options such as;

  Good, very good, extremely good, bad. These kinds of survey options make it seem you only want to get a positive reply. In this case, the ideal and unbiased survey options should be; **Good, Very good, Bad, very bad.**
- **Text limit:** When using an open survey, the ideas your users provide may be very useful to you as they are allowed to pour out their minds directly. However, the length of these replies can be so long that it delays the survey assessments process. To ensure that you get to read all replies on time and start working on them as soon as possible, always place a limit to the number of text allowed in the text box. You want to place a limit to what they

can write so you don't get a whole textbook as a survey reply.
- **Length of your survey:** The longer your survey is, the less likely you are to get users participating until the end. Make sure to keep your survey as quick and snappy as possible so it doesn't start getting boring or time consuming.

Tools for creating surveys online

1. **Google Forms:** You can create your surveys using Google forms. It is both easy and fast to create.
   To create Google forms;
   - Login to your account on Google and click on the drive option
   - Also access you drive through this link https://drive.google.com/drive/my-drive
   - Click on **my drive** drop down menu.
- Click on **Google forms** from this drop down menu or select **more** to access **Google forms** from the next options menu.
- This will take you to a form creation page. Enter the title of the form and its description on the upper part of the form.

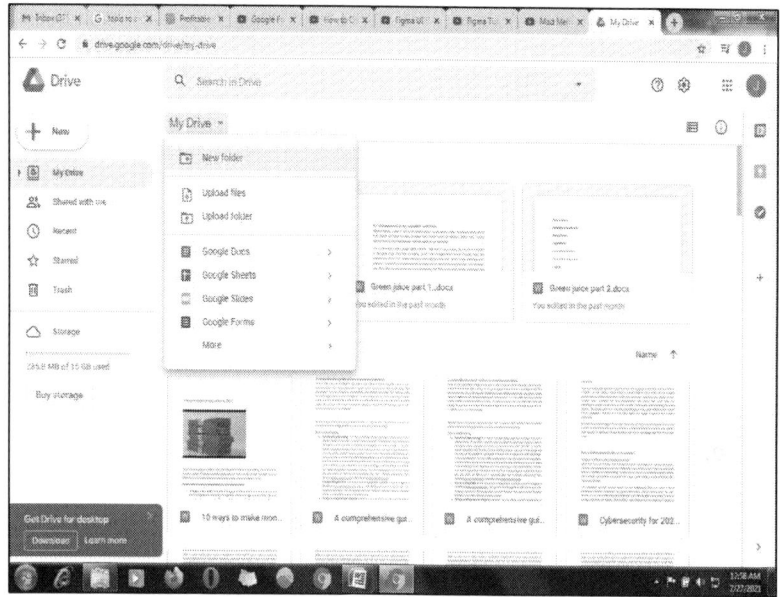

- On the lower part, you can select the type of answer you want to get by clicking on the drop down menu on the right and choosing from the list.

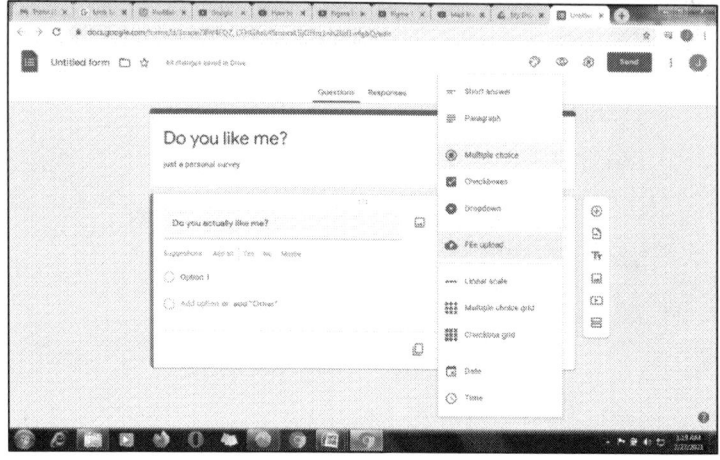

- You can add more questions to your form by clicking on the duplicate icon below the form creation page.
- Enter your question and set all other options.
- Click **send** when you are through. Now you can send to email addresses you might have collected or to your social media platforms. You can also click on the link icon to get the link of the form. Copy this link and paste it on platforms such as a website, a Facebook page/group, a forum or under a YouTube video.
- You can access your survey information by refreshing your Google drive and clicking on the form you just created. Click **responses** when the form opens. Here, you can see detailed information about the survey.

There are quite a number of other tools you can use for your surveys. Some of them include;

- ProProfs Survey maker (https://www.proprofs.com/survey/create-a-survey/)
- Surveymonkey (https://www.surveymonkey.com/)
- Surveyplanet (https://surveyplanet.com/)

Involving colleagues, stakeholders and partners in the design process

In order not to make your colleagues, business partners and your employers feel neglected, you have to involve them in the design process. It is true that you have to keep the user in mind while creating the digital product but other people's opinions matter too. Your product is meant to also make profit for your business partners and employers just as it is also meant to serve the customers better. Ask your colleagues what they think about your product. They could as well be the first users and help to modify the product until it is released into the market for other users. Why this is important is because you can also seek advice from fellow professionals in the field when you encounter a challenge. Your surveys should also not be for your users or target audience only but also for these set of individuals so you can get answers from all round.

How different individuals might use the product or service

Not all users will use the digital product in the same way. It is important to take note of this as it helps create a product that maintains equality among all users. Some might access the product from their mobile phones while others on their computer, tablet or iPad. Your product should meet all user needs regardless of their position.

One on one interviews

This is a way to get direct and live answers to your research questions. To do this, you have to find a few target users from your target audience. This way, you don't have to survey tens of thousands of users as you can get all the answers you need from these interviews.

Chapter 4

Brainstorming

Compiling your research and putting them together

Once you have your research materials, you can take all the data and start working with it. Gather all the ideas gotten from all the surveys and interviews and think of a way to put all of them into the product design.

The next step after your research is brainstorming to come up with solutions to the problems gotten from the survey. Remember, the UX designer's aim is solving the problem and obstacles users face in order to make their experience better. Brainstorming is usually done among a group of people who share ideas and work together to solve the problem. The research, which is aimed at finding the problems users face and how to better solve these problems, is the trigger for brainstorming.

Brainstorming helps you come up with creative ideas and different ideas from various people participating in the brainstorming session.

Tips to have a great brainstorming session;

- Get individuals who are professionals in the same field.
- Welcome all ideas since it is an event of sharing ideas. There should be no criticism of any ideas.
- Make the goals of the brainstorming session known to the participants so ideas can be directed toward achieving that purpose.
- Record all ideas and compile them together. This way you get to choose the best.
- The duration of the brainstorming session should not be too long. 60 to 120 minutes is ok however, it can be longer depending on the situation.
- Each group should not be more than 10 persons. Can be lesser if possible. The fewer the participants in a group brainstorming session, the more they can communicate better. Share the people into groups in case there are more people.
- Each participant should have a paper and a pen to jot down points.
- All ideas should be recorded as they serve as references.

- Stimulate the participants with things such as "putting on your thinking hats"
- There are a lot of creative brainstorming strategies you can always choose from to make your session more effective. They include; Walt Disney's creative strategy, Six Thinking Hats and Scamper.

Drafting diagrams of proposed user steps

After the brainstorming, the next step to take is to put down diagrams for the project. Your ideas will help you do this. Here you just make a rough sketch of how the pages of the project will link to one another. This is to give you an idea on how to build your UX design to make the product as easy as possible to the user. This will be illustrated better below.

Drafting wireframes

Wireframes are the first diagrams you put down to have an idea of your product pages interface. For your product, you need to create wireframes for each page the user scrolls to on your product. The content of your wireframes include how contents are displayed on the page, how the page, how the page should be organized and what functions should be made available. In this process, you also get to decide where to position your elements, buttons, social media handles and so on.

Your wireframe is solely based on your user research. This means that you decide how to draft your wireframe from the information you have gotten from your survey. The wireframe is particularly important because it is the first example picture of what the final product will look like. This is the first blueprint you follow all through your design journey and all decisions will be made to fit into this plan. Wireframes are not meant to be beautiful. In fact, wireframes are usually very rough and silly so don't worry if your wireframes look like a kindergarten's first attempt at writing. Below is the first wireframe for the social media giant – Twitter.

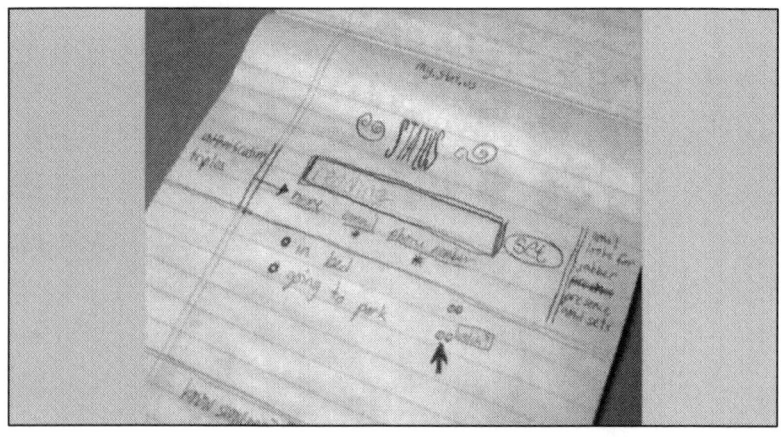

Tools you need for your wireframes;

- Pen and paper for starters.
- Your research.

You can also use a computer for your wireframes however it is much easier creating your wireframes with just a pen and paper. This is to make your skeletal sketch much easier and allow you to get as messy as possible so you can bring out all your ideas.

Creating a Prototype

These are advanced wireframes. As a UX/UI designer, your next step after drafting the wireframe (a basic design of the product) is to proceed to create a prototype (an advanced design of the product). This advanced design's visual is more detailed and interactive.

Prototypes should include colors, pictures, animations and most of the content that will be on the final product. In summary, a prototype is the closest representation of the end product.

A prototype is the best example to show your client how the end product of the design will look like.

Prototypes is usually a joint work of both the UI and UX designer because it will include buttons, colors and pictures to make the work look as good as possible.

Chapter 5

Bringing the UI designer into the picture

The UI designer comes in when it is time to create things the user needs to communicate with the software such as buttons, search fields and other functions.

Things a good UI design should include;

- **Easily accessible functions:** a good UI design should have all the user needs to operate the product readily available and very easy to find. There are thousands of choices to choose from and if a user decides to use your product, it had better be worth the time or else they can literally bolt out the moment they cannot find what they are looking for. Your search box, toolbar, help option, menu and every other tool a user needs should be placed at places that are easily accessible.
- **Sticking to a particular style:** the pages should be similar to each other in a way that the user always knows where to find a button or function. This earns your users trust and

gives them the assurance that they would always find a particular button at a particular place. This can save them time and energy and make them continue using your product.

- **Equality:** Your UI design should ensure that all users could use your device from all devices without much hassle. You should create both a mobile and desktop product so those using a mobile can still get all the features available to other users. Some users may have medical conditions such as color blindness and so on. Your product should meet all these needs through your UI design such that your users enjoy all features regardless of their conditions.
- **Clarity:** make your users clear about their progress in your product. During a transaction process for instance, make your users go from one page to another in a step-by-step process so they will be clear about where they are in the process.
- **Give feedback for user actions:**
Clicking on a button and not getting a response or visible feedback can be frustrating and be a total turn off for a user. Your UI

design should give the users feedback on any action they make.

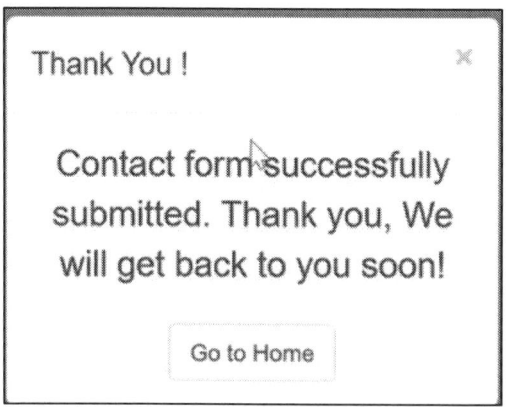

- **Use easily recognizable icons or message directives:** your users should know what an icon stands for. You can also create a display message that tells the user what the icon or button stands for. This will make navigation on your site easier for the user.
- **Placing important functions first:** your most important functions should be the first to be accessed by the user. Sometimes, users just want to search for a service or product from your app or website and do not care about signing up for a newsletter subscription. Therefore, it may be somewhat annoying to see a subscription button display first.

- **Simplicity:** do not create designs that end up giving your users a hard time to use. Your designs should be as easy and straightforward as possible.
- **Keep your users in control of their actions:**

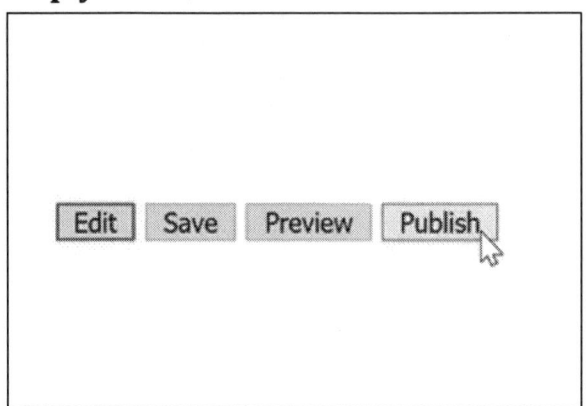

Users do not like to be held down with too many rules and restrictions. Your users should be able to be in control of what they want to do with your site. This freedom will make them freer to use your product. They should also be able to reverse their action when they want to.

Chapter 5

Implementation and Design

Front and back end developers help bring the goals set by the UX teams into reality. The product will only function after this.

Frontend development and its languages

Now that the visuals and user experience has been defined by the UX and UI designers, it's time to bring these definitions to reality. This is the stage where the front-end designers come in with the development skills. These skills include knowledge in the design languages such as HTML, CSS and JavaScript. These languages are used by the front-end developers to bring the app or web page to life.

Overview on HTML, CSS and JavaScript

HTML

Hypertext Markup Language is a worldwide accepted language for use in web design. These set of rules are used to create texts, fonts, colors and hyperlinks in web pages. HTML is usually backed by other technologies such as CSS and JavaScript.

CSS

Cascading style sheets are used to beautify web pages and also add some advanced styles and effects. The layout of the web page, its display on different devices, fonts, colors and pictures are functions of the CSS language.

JavaScript

JavaScript on the other hand is a programming language that empowers the web page to perform more than just display texts and fancy styles. JavaScript makes it possible for web pages to interact with the user and perform certain tasks such as refreshing a page automatically, moving objects across the web page and changing its display.

HTML is for documents, CSS is for the style and beauty while JavaScript is for the page interaction and activities. All three languages are used by the front-end developers to bring the interaction and beauty of the product to life.

These professionals however work closely with the UX and UI designers. They tell if the designs and functions being sampled can actually be made possible.

Backend Development

On the other side of the development is the backend development team, which focuses on the server side and database of the product. When you open an app or webpage, a server located somewhere on earth responds to you. This server powers the app or website to respond to your request. Without a backend development, commands placed by the user cannot receive responses. In other words, actions users make from the frontend of the web page or the application cannot be processed without a backend development in place.

Backend uses programming languages such as Java, PHP, C++, Python and C#.

Chapter 6

Testing

Qualitative and quantitative user research

These are research methods used to get feedback from users. A qualitative research is one that involves the experience of the user. This type of research is usually done when a moderator watches how the user reacts when using the product. Quantitative research on the other hand involves the numerical analysis from polls and general statistics. These terms are used to classify usability testing. Some usability testing can decide to go for a qualitative or quantitative testing.

Usability testing

Usability testing is getting real people to try out your product and actually use it. This is to make room for improvement in the product in order to make it perfect for the general market. A good product is known by user testing.

User testing is very important because as a designer, you might not see things the way the users see it. The ultimate goal of a usability testing is to get honest feedback to help the designers improve on the product. This is why you should test your products with more strangers.

Tips to getting a good usability testing

- Build a connection with the user and make them feel comfortable.
- Try to avoid the **word** testing as much as possible in order not to encounter trust issues.
- You don't need to test your product with a thousand users. Just a few would do. This way you can prevent the usability testing from becoming boring to you. It is true that people are different from each other but in this case, everything you need to know about your product, how people use it, improvements you need to make and so much more can be gotten from the first 4 or 5 user tests. This test method varies however if your test is one that is targeted to get a majority vote. When the test is about numbers, you can allow tests between more users.
- Do not make the usability test more like an interview where you ask the users too many questions. Try as much as possible to make

the testing more natural and less artificial. This is the way to get honest feedback.

Types of usability testing

1. In-person/Observant usability testing

This is a type of test where the moderator is present with the user. Below are various in-person usability testing types.

- **Guerilla testing:** This has been in use for quite a long time and can easily pass as the easiest testing method. In this method, you simply have to go to a place or a social gathering where you can get to meet other people. It could be a coffee shop, a pub or even a club. In this type of testing, you have to be very social to make the user as comfortable as possible with you as possible before bringing in the product for testing. You can choose your participants randomly here and get them motivated by promising them a little gift after the test is over. You can only use this article when the product is one that can be operated by the majority of users. In the case of a product such as; a trading software or photo design tool that requires some skills, you may have to try out other testing methods.

- **Lab Testing:** This is usually done in a lab environment. In this type of testing, the user is made to use the product while being studied to see how they use the product. In this type of testing, an unseen individual usually sits in a room opposite the user's to take note of some things such as facial reactions and body posture are also recorded to get the full details of how users felt using it. Lab testing comes with a lot of advantages, which includes getting deep information about how users felt while using the product. However, Lab usability testing can make users act artificially as they are not in their natural environment and sometimes, it doesn't help knowing that you are being watched.
- **Eye tracking:** in this type, the main focus is the eyes of the users as they reveal all needed to know by the observers.

2. Remote Usability testing

In this type of testing, the user performs the test from their natural environment without having someone watching from over their shoulder. Note that a remote usability testing can be moderated or not.

- **Session recording:** this is a way to get users to test the product in their natural environment by recording the whole session. This type of testing gives users freedom to actually do things themselves.
- **Phone interviews:** this time of testing involves testing the product from any part of the world while being directed by moderator on a video or voice call.

Iterative testing

This is a way to constantly improve on a product as it is being designed and tested. Iterative testing also uses usability tests to make these constant and little improvements on the product. These little improvements usually sum up in the long term and make the product much better. Iterative testing can begin at early stages of the product or when it is in use by users. Making little changes on a product may not be noticed by users already using the product but often make the experience of the user and the general quality of the product better.

Advantages of Iterative testing

- **Changes happen gradually:** this is very important because changing the whole appearance and navigation of a product may affect its users, which can lead to loss of users and can be bad for business. The new upgrade may come with a terrible user experience or an unattractive visual. These constant and little changes make it possible to transform the product to a new upgrade while maintaining the trust and patronage of the user.
- **It reduces cost:** it would have cost a fortune to redesign the whole product but with these little changes, you are able to avert that cost.
- **Easy to discover negative changes:** you can easily know what changes have affected the product negatively and easily solve them because they are usually small ones.

Steps to making a good iterative testing

- Always make changes to improve the product overall user experience or user interface. Your changes should be to serve the users better and not worse.

- Start your test as early as possible so you can identify issues early and begin making improvements so you can deliver a quality product as early as possible.
- Your changes should be little and easily acceptable by users and not big changes that may cause deliberations.

Signs of a good UX design

A good UX design is an attribute any product should have. The rate at which users stay or exit a web page or an app is dependent on the experience they get from using it.

There are quite a lot of attributes a UX design should include and some of them are listed below;

1. **Easy navigation:** a good user makes it very easy for users to navigate through the product without encountering obstacles.

2. **Product Smoothness**: when a product flows as smoothly when used and responds very quickly to instructions by the user, it is said to have a good user experience.

3. **Simplicity:** adding too many functions to your product makes it too complex and this may do more harm than good to your UX design. Simplicity is a sign of a good UX design.
4. **Less focused on sales and monetization:** A product that is too focused on sales is often a turn off for users. Trust is immediately lost once users encounter too much ads on a web page or app. These monetization tactics should be done in a way that the user still finds the information needed without too much interruption.
5. **Responsive and Friendly on all devices:** A good UX design is compatible with mobile, tablet and desktop. This all device friendly attribute makes your product more dynamic and useful to a lot of users. With the increase of mobile users over desktop and tablet combined, it has become necessary to always include this into every UX design.
6. **Load speed:** the rate at which a web page or app loads is a way to measure the UX design. A good UX design makes pages load faster.

Signs of a good UI design

Since the UX designs work hand in hand with the UI design, it is important to have a good UI design also as it can thwart the effort of the UX designer and other developers in the product.

Signs of a good UI design include;

1. **Attractiveness**

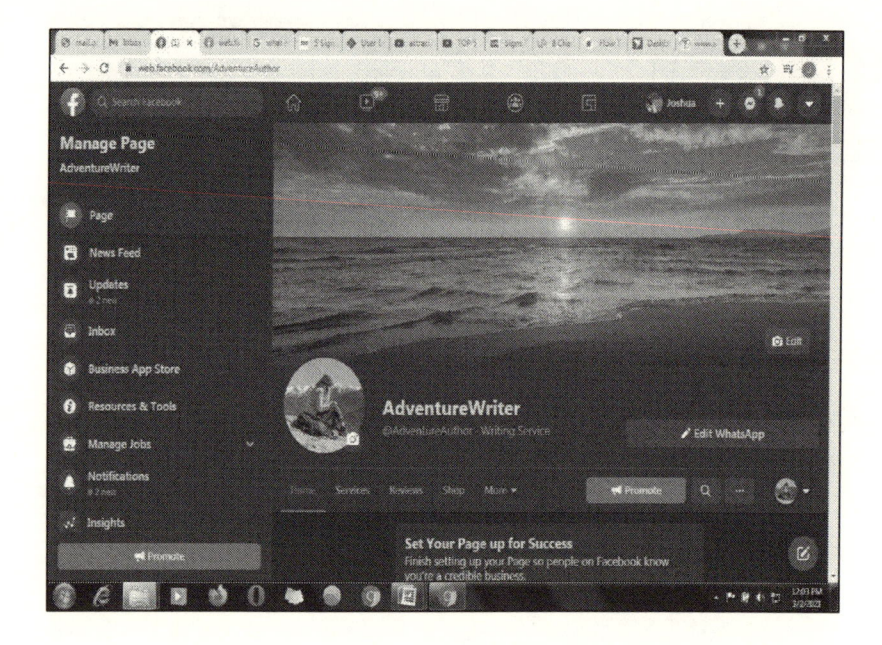

A UI design should first make sure to be attractive to the eyes. A good-looking web page or app is the first impression a user gets from it.

2. **Clear and straightforward:** users should not have to wonder what certain things in your product mean. Icons, texts, buttons and functions should have a clear and straight meaning for easy understanding.
3. **Responsiveness:** waiting so long for a page to load is a turn off to a user and they may even cause immediate exit. A product that loads all the pictures, functions and complete interface in very little time signifies a good interface.
4. **Availability of vital information**

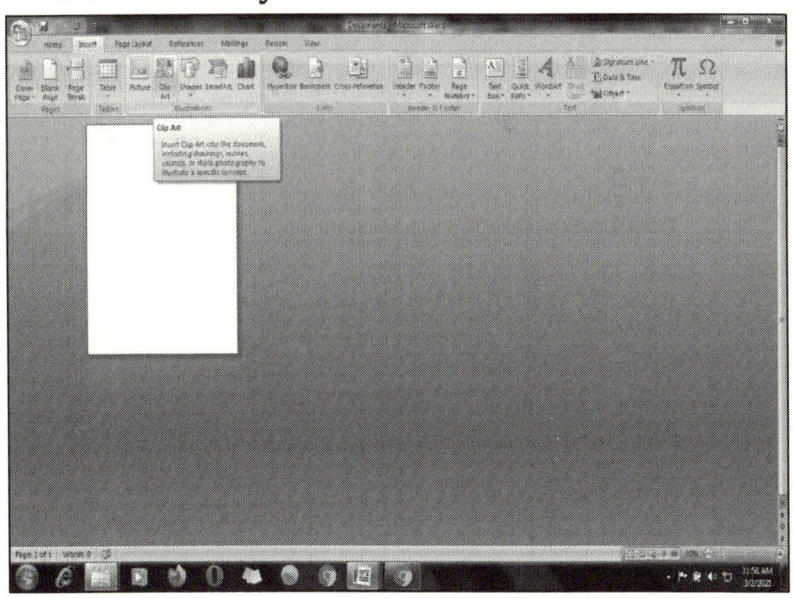

Information users might need while using your product should be made available at easily accessible places. This is one good sign of a good UI design. Users should not have to scroll over the whole page to get some of this vital information. Your search bar, menu button and so many others should be located at nearby places.

Chapter 7

Designing the ideal digital product

Making users the center of your design using UCD

Every product should be created with the users as the main focus. Sometimes, business individuals and stakeholders make the mistake of building the product mainly because of financial gain. This ends up having a bad experience for the user, which eventually leads to a bad business.

On the other hand, individuals who build their products from scratch with the user in mind and seek ways on how to satisfy the customer first eventually make profit while also satisfying their users.

A way to always keep the user in mind during the development of every product is UCD.

User centered design (UCD) is a design process whereby designers make the users the center of their design. In other words, designers implementing this method, focus on ways to build their product to meet the user's needs.

The fact is that designing an ideal digital product is basically putting the users before other players.

UCD design method uses iterative testing. What this means, is testing the product at every stage of the design process. These tests are conducted using different methods and the results are used to improve the product.

A UCD can be at more expense to the product design. However, it is the only way to get the product that would better serve the users. It is the duty of the UX and UI designers to explain to the business and stakeholders that this is in fact worth it.

In user center information, the user needs comes before the business goals.

Taking a mobile first strategy

As the mobile market share worldwide has now become bigger than the desktop, tablet market combined, designers, business individuals, and companies have started taking the mobile first strategy.

A mobile first strategy means creating a mobile version of a product before other versions. This is very important in today's world. It is a very high probability that your digital product will be accessed through a mobile device.

A few years ago, designers created a desktop version of a product first then later created a mobile version. This is understandable because it was at a time where access to the internet was mainly done through mobile devices.

In the world we live in today, designers are expected to create a mobile version before creating other versions. In fact, designers do not have to create different versions anymore. Through responsive design, the product can be accessed from different devices with ease.

Responsive design is a type of UI design capable of adjusting to all screen sizes in a smooth way such that the content and all information of the product is displayed on a mobile just as it would in a desktop. An advantage of this type of design is that it allows the designers to focus on one design rather than trying to focus on several designs at the same time.

Focusing on quality rather than quantity

The success of a digital product is not in its quantity but its quality. Users do not want to know how many pages you may have lined up to show them. They are more concerned about getting the information they need very fast and easily. This is the quality we talk about.

Questions designers should ask include; does the product provide its promises? Is it easy to use and can users call it authentic? These will make designers see things from the perspective of the users and make them see the importance of quality over quantity. Of course, the problem may most times come from other stakeholders in the project. It is the duty of the designer to point these things out and make them understand.

The importance of quality of quantity cannot be overemphasized. Below is a list of some importance of a quality over quantity in UX and UI designs;

- **Quality brings good patronage:** with a good design and the right content, which makes up a quality product, you focus little on promoting the product as it gets good patronage. This is because promotion of qua-

lity products is also done by previous users who might have found it helpful.
- **Quality designs empower improvement:** focusing on quality gives the designers more time to focus on improving the product and also reveal new ways to make the product better serve individuals.
- **Easier to operate:** a quality product is easier to operate as it is well arranged and gives the user access to useful information at all times.
- **Trust:** a quality product design trust among business partners, stakeholders, colleagues while also building a good reputation with its users.
- **Good reference:** a quality product is a good reference for a designer to help win future clients and more jobs.

Tips to build quality designs

1. **Knowing your users:** your product is obviously built to serve users better and solve problems. Knowing the potential users of your product matters in building quality. If your users will be students, it is important to take note of the attributes that would make your product quality enough for them. Your

product should solve the problems it was made to solve and bring improvement in the lives of its users.
2. **Limit the distractions:** a quality product is not one that immediately starts bombarding its users with distractive contents as soon as the user logs in to use it. This will create fear and distrust in the user such that it would be difficult to patronize the product next time.
3. **Avoid confusing content:** designers usually do this to make the product bulkier. When the webpage or app is choked up with too much information, it becomes difficult for the user to make choices. This overwhelming feeling eventually makes the user unsure of the next action to take. This usually happens when there are too many buttons in the pages of a product. It eventually leads to confusion and when users become confused, they flee.
4. **Make the content easy to find and read:** the size of texts, colors and others should be easy to access.

Information architecture (IA)

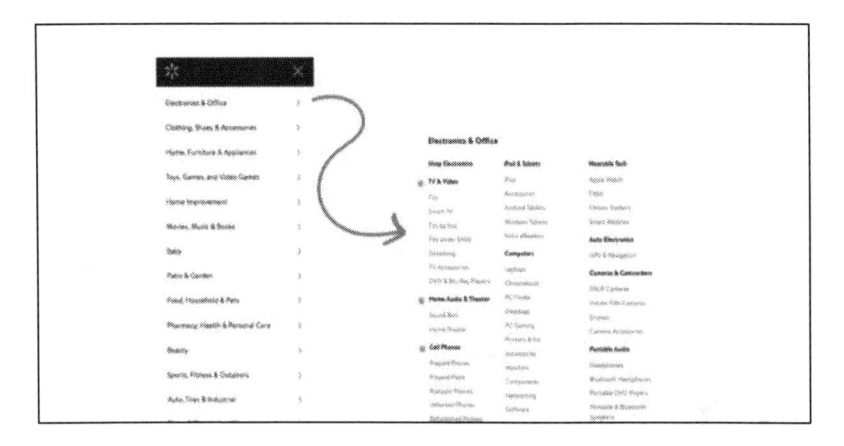

This is the arrangement and structuring of content in a product design.

The way content and functions are arranged in a website or app is vital to its success. A well-arranged design makes it easier for users to browse through and operate your product.

Information architecture is closely related to UX design as both focus in arrangement of content to make user experience better.

The Ancient Egyptians were famous for bringing this idea into the modern world through their excellent arrangement skills usually used in their libraries.

A product without proper IA is almost totally useless to users especially in a world where there are thousands of other places users could go to get the same information or service they need.

Just like building architects, information architects focus solely on the structure of the product. These professionals make information finding easy majority of hidden content will be found if the product has a great IA

Importance of a good Information Architecture

- **Easy access to information:** This is the main aim of IA in every design and it is ensuring that users spend less time looking for information they need.
- **More patronage:** Good information makes the users spend more time on the product and consume more information due to its easy information finding nature. This also gives you an advantage because the longer a user stays using the product; the more likely they are to purchase something, click on an ad or even come back next time.
- **SEO Advantage:** a good Information Architecture can help rank the website high

on search engines and bring more traffic for your web pages.

Why you should be a UX and UI designer

In the course of your reading so far, you must have noticed that UX and UI design indeed differ from each other and yet work closely together in the design process. Now the question is, which should you learn in order to be at an advantage?

The answer is obvious. You should be both. Some may tell you to focus on just one at a time and learn the other but you really don't have to limit yourself because both professions are different from each other. Learning both skills gives you an advantage over several other professionals. It means you will be able to perform the roles of the UX designer and still put them into work in the UI design.

Below are some reasons why being a UX and UI designer is so important;

- **More opportunities:** a professional with both skills gets more job opportunities and more clients.
  Think of it this way; you are a client looking for a designer for your project and you come across a professional's profile and the descri-

ption of the profile is "I am a **UX** and **UI designer**". Would you hire the individual or not? Of course, you would. Aside from very large companies with advanced designs, most companies now look for individuals with both UX and UI skills and even though they have a specialist in one of the fields, they'll still choose a professional with both skills to complete the team. Nevertheless, you can easily switch to one of the terms if the need arises.

- **Better understanding of the project:** you get to view the design from both points and it is easy to take your UX research and apply UI design to it. This makes the whole design project easy, as there is no need to explain the whole design requirement to another person.

- **A wider spectrum of skills:** you probably guessed right. A person with both skills comes with more problem solving capabilities. This more ideas and more ways to better serve the customers come to the team.

Chapter 8

The user Interface

How graphic design knowledge helps in UI design

One important skill in building attractive User Interfaces is graphic design. However, there is more to what the graphic design skills do in UI design other than make the product attractive.

Graphic designers focus on creating static visual elements in the product while UI design takes these visual elements and focus on how the user will interact with them. User interfaces also focus on how these visual elements will respond to the users. The fact here is that the graphic design is the first step in user interface design.

These skills used in UI design find most of their roots in graphic design principles. If you have graphic design skills, you can easily transfer them to UI design however, there are a few more skills you would need to learn and some include coding languages such as CSS and HTML.

Having knowledge in graphic design as a UI designer makes you stand out from other designers in this rapidly growing and competitive design world.

Using breathtaking images

It isn't just about the type of website or app you are creating as a designer. The fact is that great images are important to attracting and keeping users entertained. In fact, users will naturally feel a product is very good once they love the picture they see. Good images can keep users glued to your product a little longer than they should have if there were no images.

With good images, you only need to say little to make users understand your point. It is true that images tell a thousand words and in this case, it tells the user a thousand words about the product. Good Images can inspire and motivate the user and also reflect the purpose of the product.

Images change the mood of its viewers and this can be used as an advantage by UI designers. An image such as the one above will immediately put the user in a calm mood that ushers him/her into the next action to take on the website.

Effects of colors and font

Colors and fonts are a crucial part of the product. These contents play a crucial role in the overall user experience.

Colors

Organizing colors is important in creating a good UI design. There are many terms regarding this area, which include; seven elements of color, color psychology, the golden ratio and general color rules.

Designers use colors to beautify, show trust and evoke emotions in users. For instance, the most widely used color - blue is used in so many websites and apps because it represents trust, reliability and is a good representation of innovation.

The numbers do not lie. An interesting fact to know is that the majority of people worldwide prefer the color blue to other colors hence they would respond positively to it.

The color blue is the world's favorite color. It is also the favorite color of the United States and you wonder why this is so. Well, a color brings calm and serenity to the viewer. The site of the blue sky and sea on a bright day brings with it a different kind of calmness.

Based on these facts, blue is the highly recommended color to add to every design project.

Fonts

The fonts of your content also matters in the overall use experience of the user. This is the graphical display of texts and it is so important that it can be the reason why users read or do not read it.

Users do not want discomfort and would not spend much time taking in content that is stressful to their eyes. Your content should be bold and relaxing to the eyes. In addition, it is very likely that your users will access your product through a mobile device, you don't want them pinching the screen, and struggling to read what so much time and energy have been spent on writing.

Responsive and adaptive design

One of the duties of the UI designer is to make the product accessible through various devices. Earlier, we talked about taking a mobile first strategy using Responsive design. Now we are going to also talk about adaptive design as they apply to UI design.

Choosing between responsive and adaptive design may be hard for some designers as they both come with their advantages and disadvantages.

Responsive design

This is having one design, which works on all devices and browsers fitting into all of them perfectly. Responsive web design is created in a way that the content is like liquid, which simply changes smoothly and takes the form of the vessel it is poured into. These types of designs generally use components such as; Flexible layout, flexible media and media queries to give the design responseveness to different browsers and screen sizes.

Advantages

- Easier to implement.

- Requires less time and effort.
- Can be easily updated.
- Responsive design websites are more SEO friendly.
- Responsive design doesn't care much about devices but is a great solution to different device layout.

Disadvantages

- Some features and buttons created for desktop versions may not display exactly on mobile devices.
- Loading time may vary across various devices.
- Structure of the design may not be the same as other devices, which may scatter some content such as ads.

Adaptive design

This type of design focuses on creating different layouts to best fit different devices. Adaptive design is time and money consuming as you would have to create various designs for different devices. However, it can be very effective for good user experience.

What adaptive design does is that it selects the best layout once it detects the device and displays that to the user. For instance if you are accessing the site using a smartphone, an adaptive design will simply display a mobile layout to you.

Advantages

- Brings specific versions for specific devices.
- Pages load quite fast.

Disadvantages

- Requires more time and finance to create versions for several devices.
- Some users with devices such as tablets and iPads may be left out of the process since the adaptive design may have created only desktop and smartphone layouts.
- Adaptive designs don't usually do well in SEOs.

Responsive and adaptive design may work for different individuals however; it is clear that responsive design has quite a lot of edge over adaptive design. It is also the most used type of design since designers, business people and companies just want a product that would serve all users regardless of the device they are on.

Creating equal accessibility to all users

Users come with various differences and it is important to take note of them. Some may be victims of color blindness while others may have short sight and so on. Your UI design should consider this to create equal accessibility to all of them.

This is a major problem most products face. Your product will only be fully successful if it can be accessed by users from all parts of the world and at any time, they want to. Creating a product and limiting its accessibility only to China or the UK will diminish its potential.

Individuals with limitations also have the right to use your product and discriminating people based on their disabilities is unruly. Products should seek ways to serve all users including those with special needs.

Including this in the design process from start makes your product meet its ultimate goal, which is to serve people.

Some areas to take into consideration to deal with this accessibility problem include;

- **Visuals:** This limitation includes all kinds of sight problems and all kinds of blindness, which also includes color blindness.
- **Location:** your product should be accessed by more than just the people in one location but across different countries of the world.
- **Device compatibility**: your designs should be accessed by users on all devices and not just desktop and smartphone users.

Chapter 9

The Kaizen concept

What is the Kaizen Concept?

Kaizen is a Japanese concept, which has been found very useful in business and generally all walks of life. Its literal meaning in English is "Constant and continuous improvement". It is a type of improvement, which happens gradually rather than all at once.

Kaizen is aimed at making things better than they were previously. These changes can be daily, weekly, monthly or yearly and are usually little ones but are usually great when put together in the long run.

We all know how difficult change can be; however, it is one thing that is constant in life. We simply cannot escape these changes from happening to us. Taking deliberate decisions to make a change and putting in action may seem hard. This is so because oftentimes, we focus on changing it all at once. Kaizen is the way to overcome this problem as we now see that little, deliberate, constant and consistent improvement can lead to a desired change in the long term.

Toyota applies this concept to their business, which is why they are the largest car producers in the world today.

Applying this to UX and UI design is one way to always stay on top of the game. It is important to note that the work never really ends for designers, as they must always improve their products every now and then. Making little changes to your design as more people use it can make a very drastic impact on the overall product in no time.

One advantage of this impact is that the users just flow with and accept it since they hardly even notice the changes. This is the way to upgrade your product without affecting the users.

Improvement through feedback

Making improvement through feedback requires getting the right feedback and an understanding of how constructive criticism can be very useful to your product. This is one reason why usability tests are very important in UX/UI design. The usability test gives you all the feedback needed to make improvement.

Feedbacks are not just constructive criticism. They can also come in very negative forms. Keep it in mind that the goal is to improve. Hence, you should ward off feedback that threatens to backtrack and destroy the motivation and progress of the design.

Working toward improvement rather than perfection

The one who seeks to improve gets the motivation to keep learning and taking simple steps but the one who seeks perfection will always find a way to put things off until tomorrow.

Seeking perfection is exhausting and it is one target that keeps many people in the game of procrastination and frustration for a long time.

Perfection to many individuals is a goal achieved by taking big steps and making hard changes. Due to the magnitude of such changes, the individuals often put it off to the future. It is therefore safe to say that perfection is the root of procrastination.

Frustration also sets in where perfection is the target due to self-set goals that are simply unattainable.

Instead of striving for perfection, have a quick strategizing and focus on improving little by little just like the age long Kaizen concept which has been implemented by some great organizations that exist today.

Perfection is also a very boring goal when achieved, as the achiever will find nothing stimulating over there.

Reasons to aim for improvement rather than perfection

- Improvement empowers learning and hard work whereas in the case of perfection, learning stops once it is achieved.
- Perfection leads to discouragement and self-regret and self-hate due to its unrealistic requirement.
- Improvement is a growth process, which can be followed by humans. It is one that follows the natural growth laws of man, of plants, animals and all the elements that make up the human world.
- Perfection is exhausting especially when a mistake is made. Improvement on the other hand embraces failure, which is actually necessary for growth. Failure is usually a step

back in improvement that allows maintenance of a good position and a very strong come back.
- Perfection is an attempt to massage the ego to make the individual feel good enough. In other words, people who seek perfection are often those with inferiority complex who think they are not good enough the way they are.
- Perfection is short lived because it feels like the end. There is not much to celebrate at the end of something. The journey is the place where the fun and the activities are.
- Perfection is a killer of creativity, enthusiasm and confidence. When you seek to be perfect, your eyes are fixed on a single goal hereby blocking your mind to new ways of solving problems and being creative. Perfection kills enthusiasm and confidence and this usually happens when the perfectionist encounters problem

In addition, a question to ask is "what happens if the perfection no longer meets the requirement of the users?"

Designers who seek perfection should always remember that we are dealing with humans who are dynamic and often unpredictable. This then brings the need to always adjust to the direction of the users.

This shows that there is nothing like perfection in a world such as this. It is always constant improvement for the better.

Conclusion

UX and UI design work together to bring the ideal design to life. For the perfect product to be brought to life, both design processes have to work with other professionals which include the frontend and back end developer who must make sure they meet the user goals of the UX designer.

A UX designer is responsible for making the user experience better. This way, the users can operate the product with ease. A UI designer makes sure to create all the interfaces the user uses to communicate with the app or website. These interfaces include buttons, options, and menu, search and input fields. The UI designers also beautify the product to make it attractive to the users.

It is important to note that one does not work without the other and companies most times do not look for just one skill but both to bring in more ideas and experience to the designs.

For this reason, you should consider learning both skills to be on a more advantageous side.

The Kaizen concept is open for the taking. Many businesses worldwide have already taken and put it into practice. It is necessary in UX design as the design process never stops but involves constant improvement to always meet the needs of the users.

About the Author

Davis Weathers is a Tech enthusiast who found his way into the world of UX/UI design. He has been in the industry for more than a decade and has therefore decided to compile his knowledge to share with those who seek help in understanding the concept of UX/UI Design.

Manufactured by Amazon.ca
Bolton, ON